Facts About the Kiwi

By Lisa Strattin

© 2019 Lisa Strattin

FREE BOOK

FREE FOR ALL SUBSCRIBERS

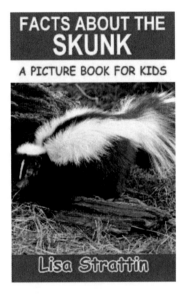

LisaStrattin.com/Subscribe-Here

BOX SET

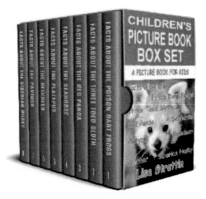

- FACTS ABOUT THE POISON DART FROGS
- FACTS ABOUT THE THREE TOED SLOTH
  - FACTS ABOUT THE RED PANDA
  - FACTS ABOUT THE SEAHORSE
  - FACTS ABOUT THE PLATYPUS
  - FACTS ABOUT THE REINDEER
  - FACTS ABOUT THE PANTHER
- FACTS ABOUT THE SIBERIAN HUSKY

LisaStrattin.com/BookBundle

Contents

INTRODUCTION

The Kiwi is native to the forests and jungles of New Zealand.

They are thought to be related to the ostrich and the emu, making them the smallest member of this family of birds. Like it's larger cousins, they are unable to fly due to their small wing span and heavy weight. They spend their life foraging for food on the forest floor.

CHARACTERISTICS

There are many different species of Kiwi, but all of them are found living in the forests of New Zealand.

The Kiwi is the national bird and icon of New Zealand. In fact, the native people there are often also called Kiwis! The Kiwi also appears on many flags and symbols across the islands.

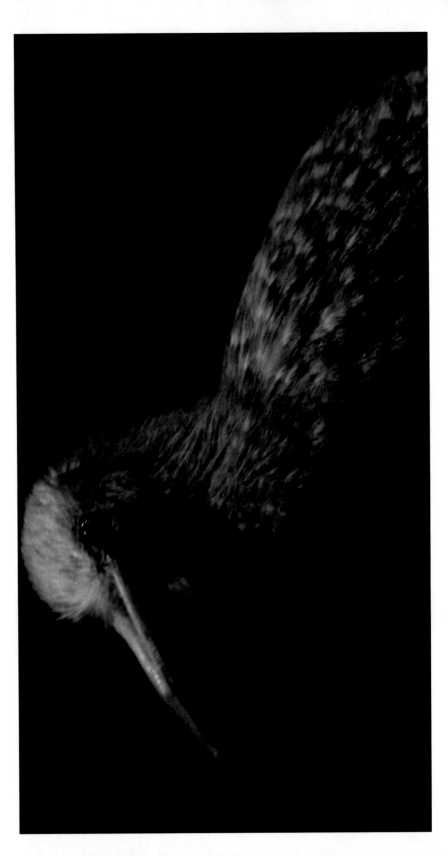

APPEARANCE

The kiwi is a brown, fuzzy, flightless bird. They have a very long beak that is about a third the length of their entire body.

REPRODUCTION

The eggs of the kiwi weigh about one pound. They lay one of the largest eggs of all birds! Because of their size, when the new birds hatch, the mother does not have to care for the hatchling at all.

LIFE SPAN

Kiwi birds live for an average of 8 to 12 years in the wild.

SIZE

Adult Kiwi can be up to 17 inches tall with very short wings, even though they cannot fly. They weigh about 7 pounds or so.

HABITAT

Although Kiwi birds are generally solitary animals, they are known to live in pairs for at least a part of their lives. These couples mate only with each other and the female is usually larger than the male, and the female is generally the dominant bird of the pair.

They are nomads. They move around a lot instead of staying in one place. They dig burrows which they sleep in and then move on to another spot and build a new burrow the next night. The only exception is when the bird is nesting to lay eggs. The female lays an average of 5 eggs per clutch which take almost 3 months to hatch. The male is the one who incubates the eggs for most of the time.

DIET

Kiwi is an omnivorous bird and eats a variety of both plants and animals. They mainly hunt for worms, insects and spiders but also will eat fruits and berries, generally those that are on the forest floor. They use the long beak to rummage through the foliage on the ground in search of food.

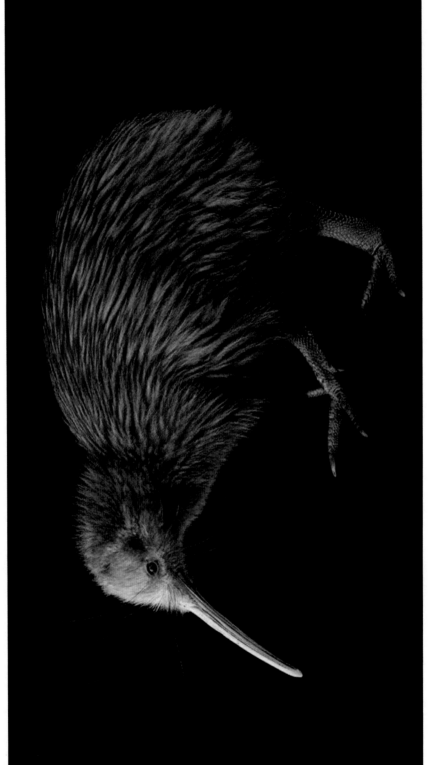

ENEMIES

Before the introduction of animals such as cats and dogs to their home range, these birds roamed New Zealand in great numbers. It is since humans settled in these areas, with their pets, that the bird's numbers have rapidly declined.

In recent years the Kiwi has become endangered, mostly due to predators like dogs, cats, rats, ferrets and weasels which hunt the kiwi and eat its eggs. The kiwi is almost helpless against these threats. Today there are believed to only around 200 Kiwis left in the wild!

SUITABILITY AS PETS

Since these birds are endangered, it is not a good idea to try to keep one as a pet. They would be considered an exotic pet as they are only found native to New Zealand, so you would be required to have an exotic pet license – if that is even possible. You might be able to see them in your local zoo, if there is a habitat there.

COLOR ME

COLOR ME

COLOR ME

COLOR ME

COLOR ME

COLOR ME

COLOR ME

Please leave me a review here:

LisaStrattin.com/Review-Vol-282

For more Kindle Downloads Visit Lisa Strattin
Author Page on Amazon Author Central

amazon.com/author/lisastrattin

To see upcoming titles, visit my website at
LisaStrattin.com– most books available on Kindle!

LisaStrattin.com

FREE BOOK

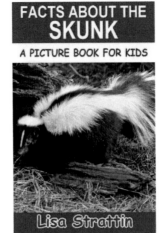

Made in the USA
Las Vegas, NV
06 March 2023

68610988R10026